The Poetic
Melody

Ms. Arpita Roy

ISBN 979-8-89026-493-0

This book is soulfully dedicated to my late father **Mrinal Ranjan Roy** who loved and considered me most in the entire universe and my dear mother
Smt. Manabi Roy.

Preface

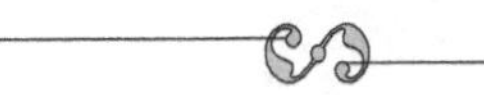

First and foremost I would like to express my enormous gratitude to the entire universe. This universal journey is incredible indeed. In my first English poetry book, "The Poetic Melody", I have written about different shades of life those touch my tiny heart.

This book is about the universe, self-help, humanity, peace, science, nature, love, break-up, friendship and many more shades of life. This book has a poetic melody. Hopefully that can be heard by your inner core.

I try to write all being truthful and unbiased. In my creative journey I sincerely try to sense poetic justice. As an author I absolutely don't have any intent to hurt anyone. I write all based on how I embrace the universe in my heart. This universal journey is always unique for each of us. As an author I wish to be a tiny contributor to the universe and beyond.

You can share your feedback at: **writenow2arpita@gmail. com**

Best wishes,
Arpita Roy

Contents

An Eternal Writer

The lady tries to hear the unheard voice.

She tries to realize the truth by removing all the deceptive noise.

She tries to see the performers on the invisible stage.

She tries to reveal the truth of the uncovered phase.

She tries to break the untouched cage.

She wants to be the voice of the voiceless.

So she empathetically keeps writing.

Most importantly she finds peace in writing.

She knows how to tug at readers' heartstrings.

Writing is her emotional flow.

She doesn't get tired to do so.

She writes to live and let live.

She writes just the way she breathes.

Her pen will never be sold.

She is kind, unbiased and bold.

She feels deeper than the sea.

Often she is fondly accompanied by a cup of tea.

She writes from dawn to dusk.

Being brutally honest, she writes all without wearing any invisible mask.

She writes to free herself and let others be free.

She wants to write until the falling of the last leaf of the maple tree.

Life has infinite shades.

She wants to write until her brain is dead.

She wants to write until the falling of the last raindrop on the window glass.

She wants to write until the clinging of the last dewdrop to the green grass.

She wants to write to let the storm of stress pass.

She wants to write until the end of the last song of the nightingale.

She writes viewing the world from a different angle.

She writes overcoming any fear.

She writes to wipe away the tears.

She wants to write in the lap of nature.

She wants to write under the snowy mountain.

She wants to write to let the people forget their pain.

She wants to write inside the mysterious caves.

She wants to write listening to the sound of the waves.

She plays with the alphabets.

She feels more alive whenever she writes.

She was born to write.

Writing is her inner light.

Writing is the best ever therapy for her.

Do you know who she is, my dear?

She is none other than an eternal writer.

The Magical Touch of Poetry

Poetry is the fountain of words flowing from our hearts.

Poetry is a dream come true in the form of deep
emotional art.

Poetry is made of the aura of our smile and tears.

Our indifference is the silent trigger.

Poetry is the most ornamental expression of any
language.

Poetry resonates with our minds' each and every wavy
phase.

Poetry can eventually cure our all the pain.

The poetic aura brings the artistic joy in our veins.

The magical touch of poetry takes us from hell to
heaven.

When the words are drawn, poetry is born.

In our inner world we deal with emotions.

In the outer world we occasionally breathe out poetic
vibes.

Poetry is one of the most powerful gifts to keep our
almost dead dreams alive.

Poetry is the divine bliss.

Poetry is the source of our inner peace.

Poetry is our last hope.

Poetry lets our real life mingle with imagination liberating the reality beyond its scope.

Poetry is the freedom of the wings of a bird.

Poetry is often the emotional amalgam of reality and dreams what once was unheard.

Poetry is the pictorial representation of the words.

In the darkness, starry poetry is the humanitarian guide.

Poetry is as beautiful as the veil of a newlywed bride.

Poetry is the blooming rose among the thorns.

Poetry is the first light of the dawn.

Poetry is an eternal journey.

Poetry is a forever mystery.

Poetry is the burning fire,

Poetry is the emotions of the wavy river,

Poetry is the smell of the wet soil.

You need a poetic escape in turmoil.

Poetry is the fragrance of the gardenia.

It's a blessing to live in a poetic euphoria.

Poetry is the warmth of literature.

Let our souls have poetic pleasure.

Though one day we all will die like the windy leaves
fallen around the tree

yet each of us will remain immortal being the living
poetry.

Let poetry be the voice of all the injustice and
grievance.

Let poetry be the soul of the romance.

Let the music of poetry on.

Let's make the world more poetic to bring peace and
happiness for our beloved daughters and sons.

Daddy

Daddy, you are always in my mind.

I'm genetically blessed to be simple and kind.

You have such an amazing gene.

You never make me feel unheard and unseen.

Daddy, you give me the strength to deal with any
stormy wind.

You make me believe, father's love is blind.

Oh daddy, please bless me not to get lost.

I feel your fatherly warmth even in the deadly frost.

Daddy, I am your loving daughter,

but sometimes it seems, you are my dear son and I'm
your beloved mother.

Just like you I bloom silently even when I suffer.

Daddy, you are the spirit of my every soulful work.

You are my insightful spark.

You are my heart's angel.

Your affection is always with me no matter whether I'm
in earthy heaven or hell.

You are nonjudgmental.

Daddy, I'm your forever little girl.

Daddy, our tears get mixed and turn into a divine pearl.

Daddy, you are my soulful smile in the midst of diabolical conspiracy.

Daddy, you are my absolute truth in the midst of the hellish lie and hypocrisy.

When I am the speaker,

you are the most avid listener.

You are the truth deep down my bones.

But daddy, why am I not getting you in phone?

Please call me soon.

In our very own daddy-daughter galaxy you are my golden sun and I'm your pearly moon.

Daddy, your heart is my most comfortable nest.

You have seen me at my worst and still encourage me to be the best.

On this planet earth I'm your most considerate guest.

But daddy, are you getting tired? Do you want to take a bit rest?

Why can't my earthy eyes see your affectionate face?

What's the mess?

Do we finally have to be separated by the inevitable call
of the last breath?

No matter what happens with us,

we must stay tuned with the eternal soul of the
universe.

I'm your heartfelt melody; you are my humming flute.

I'm your mangrove tree; you are my breathing root.

You breathe so I breathe too.

I'm alive so you are alive too.

You never make me feel all alone and blue.

You are my beloved father and a dear friend.

You stay with me till my end.

You never say me a forever goodbye.

Daddy, when death comes,

We will breathe together again with the twinkling stars
at the night sky.

Stay Loyal

Relationship is just like a blooming flower.

Relationship is wrapped in love, trust and care.

Loyalty is its holy fragrance.

A loyal lover can break the hardest fence.

A true relationship assures no cheating, no lies.

Staying loyal is the most blissful relationship advice.

No one can give the guarantee of an everlasting partnership.

But the loyal partners wouldn't have to be the passengers on the trust's sinking ship.

An honest partner doesn't get fear to hold your hand tightly in front of others.

Betrayal is a very cruel teacher.

Nowadays so many frauds are keeping multiple relationships at the same time just pretending to be the secret lovers.

Loyalty has a sacred spark.

A loyal partner doesn't let the red rose of your heart be plucked.

Loyalty is a continual phenomenon.

Loyalty prevails on heart's devotion.

The essence of loyalty is divinely pure.

An honest partner thinks about his future plan with you for sure.

An honest partner must stay with you through thick and thin.

Be with someone who is genuinely ready to accept your presence under his loyal skin.

An unfaithful partner will eventually dig your mental grave.

Be with someone who is honest enough to keep your loyal heart safe.

Even if someone betrays you, never ever betray yourself.

The worst betrayal is nothing but betraying yourself.

Always stay loyal with your authentic self.

A Soulful Creator

The lady is an avid observer.

She is a truth-seeker.

She is a mind reader.

She is a constant learner.

She is a lifetime mentor.

She is an undefeated fighter.

She is a sleepless dreamer.

Life is a roller coaster

and she is one of our most passionate co-riders.

She is our mind's mirror.

She is our brain's interrogator.

She is our wound's healer.

She is our heart-stealer.

She is our soul's sympathizer.

She is our conscience's regular visitor.

She is our source of thriller.

She always has a creative goal.

In the world of creativity she has faithfully devoted with all her heart and soul.

Whenever it comes to creative energy, she is always on top.

Her creativity resonates with the sound of the raindrops.

Her creative vibes are present in the sunny summer and the snowy winter.

When autumn leaves start to fall even then her hope for exploring creativity doesn't stop rising.

Her creative world becomes vibrantly colorful in the spring.

She is the song of a singer.

She is the painting of a painter.

She is the sporty spirit of a player.

She is an image-maker,

She is an image-breaker.

She is an enthusiastic starter.

She is a dotted finisher.

She is an instantaneous speaker.

She is an attentive listener.

She is the warrior of warriors.

She is full of creative energy.

Creativity always keeps her busy.

She has creative hormones and neurons.

She wants to live with her passion.

Who is she, my dear?

She is none other than a soulful creator.

She moulds her creative thoughts now, then and forever.

She is blessed with infinite creative liberty and imaginative power.

Mother Nature is the creator of creators.

And that lady is a beloved daughter of Mother Nature.

Stay Healthy

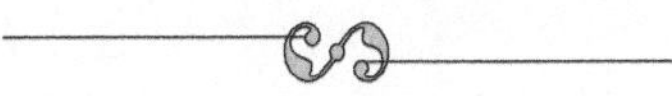

Sound health makes your life really worthy.

Anyhow try to stay healthy.

Prolonged illness is a time-bound slavery.

It's like living in a death valley.

Eat healthy, drink healthy.

Have a sound sleep.

Regularly do exercise to stay active.

Be positive.

Somewhere someone is dyeing to take one more
healthy breath.

Health is incomparably the most important wealth.

Health empowers our inner faith.

Stay blessed with a sound health.

Never neglect this priceless biological wealth.

Nothing is more precious than a healthy breath.

You can't sit for an exam feeling extremely unwell.

Then even being the most deserved candidate to stand
first, you have to fail.

To stay fit, just leave your unhealthy habits.

Your healthy body and mind are your divine blessings
that welcomes your inner spring.

Good health is your highest level of achievement.

Stay healthy to do your work assignment.

Stay healthy to enjoy your 'Me Time' beyond any
commitment.

Be strong to fight for yourself.

Stay healthy to support yourself.

Scientifically stay committed to your health to save
yourself.

Giving honest effort for staying healthy is the most
essential self-help.

Make this choice inevitable.

No need to count your wrinkles.

Your body is soulfully your holiest temple.

Stay tuned with the melodious health to smile with
your dancing dimple.

Never Leave Yourself

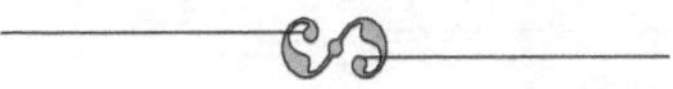

Stay blessed with your zeal and zest.

Be your heart's most important guest.

Love yourself truer than the truest.

Nothing is more soothing than being your own friend.

Mentally and physically you have to try to stay healthy
till the end.

You are a living bookshelf.

Blissfully develop a unique sense of self.

Be committed to your innermost self.

In future you will have to take part in an unknown
rally.

You never know, what will ultimately be your life's
summary?

Whatever will be will be,

You earnestly need yourself to find the pearl of peace in
the universal sea.

So just promise me,

no matter what happens with you, never leave yourself,
my dearie.

Listen Your Core

The most dangerous choice is nothing but the blind trust.

Take your time and intelligence to know the difference between love and lust.

Be your true companion.

Observe the change in the natural phenomenon.

Listen to your brain wrapped in your heart to choose a friend or a partner.

Today's lover can be tomorrow's stranger.

Today's so called friend can be just invisible in tomorrow's danger.

To sense the truth, listen to your core.

Don't get fear to walk alone on life's river shore.

To have an honest companionship, you have to be wisely choosy.

Only genuine people deserve your limited earthy time and the sacred energy.

Ugly truth may temporarily break your heart.

But in the long run acceptance of truth makes you wise
and smart.

Simplicity sensibly shines.

The more you stay simple the more you read between
the lines.

Life is a small trip.

Time on our hands is too short to weep.

Learn to value honest fellowship.

Just because you are alone, don't swallow the poison of
the fake companionship.

Be the vigilant captain of your cosmic ship.

Get Well Soon

Being severe ill, your brain and body just want to have
a bit speedy recovery.

Unbearable pain makes a sunny mind helplessly foggy.

Irrecoverable pain even wants to welcome death to get
a permanent relief

considering death is the end of all the grief

as there is no longer need to deal with any problem.

The weaker you feel the lesser chance you have to find
your inner flame.

Illness tries to swallow your mind and body.

Illness is an almost inevitable existential tragedy.

When a patient is ill, weak and pale,

A doctor comes to him just like an angel.

Illness is the fate's most helpless slavery.

Wish all the patients could have speedy recovery.

An optimistic message for all of them, 'Get well soon.

Hope to see your healthy smiles forever just like the
scintillating moon.'

Be you

People keep judging you,

objectify you.

But life has taught you, just keep going on no matter whatever result you get.

Nothing can be learned without mistake, my universal classmate.

Uncertainty prevails.

Even after giving your highest effort, you might fail.

Be committed to your innermost self always and forever.

Be your broken heart's most soothing healer.

Don't be the prisoner of people's judgments.

Keep molding your overall existence for the further betterment.

Under any circumstances choose freedom.

Plant your wounds in the field of patience to harvest the crops of wisdom.

You are your most valuable wealth.

Feel your tiny heart's warmth.

Trust your every breath.

Think for yourself.

Speak to yourself.

Build yourself.

Check yourself.

Correct yourself.

Appreciate yourself.

Validate yourself.

Embrace yourself.

Be extremely kind to yourself.

Don't be afraid to be yourself.

Unapologetically be yourself.

An original one is always more worthy than copy.

Your true self must make you feel free and happy.

Don't ever be blind to follow the crowd.

To speak the truth you don't always need to be loud.

When you are not valued,

just mentally get detached from that source of connection.

You are better off alone without dealing with any negative minded person.

Your sensitive mind always needs your affection.

Don't ever expect that life would be fair, just always be available for self-care.

Why are you seeking water whereas you yourself are the river?

Leave your emotional baggage behind for flying high just like a flight feather.

Be intelligent enough to deal with any mess.

Let your inner peace be the reflection of your eternal grace.

Nothing can make you feel more beautiful than your self-confidence.

Your universally gifted uniqueness lies in your youness.

Be you, be true and be fearless.

The Wise Mind

You are in pursuit of wisdom.

Let your mind be wise bit by bit with universal rhythm.

Know your worth very well.

Mentally get detached from any trash talk spreading negative smell.

Don't get imprisoned in criticizer's jail.

Your life depicts an unbelievable struggling tale no matter whether you succeed or fail.

Don't allow anything to let your soul be pale.

Your mind is a candle, let it be kindled.

Being alive is the most awakening dream.

Just kiss the hope's sunbeam.

Wisdom helps you to take the strategy based on your decisive stream.

You are the undefeated warrior.

Value your every drop of tear.

Don't rely on anything but your heart.

Without holding any grudge in your mind, consider all
the facts.

After fact-checking, intelligently perform any act.

To do something, you must need your own permission.

Your heart is a fountain.

Your heart doesn't let the water deem to be stagnant.

Don't allow anyone to misuse your tender heart over
and over again.

Be strong enough to breathe life accepting any pain.

Dive into your conscientious depth.

Finding your inmost self you can have your most
valuable wealth.

Be rooted so deep that you don't fear the wind.

Keep balance between emotions and intelligence to
have a wise mind.

Emotions Are Natural

My friend, you are not a robot.

Your mind has a deep emotional root.

Some people say, you are too much emotional.

Just remember, emotions are biologically normal.

Emotions are quite natural.

Emotional vibes are like the human communication signals.

In your feathery heart, I can see the beauty of an opal.

In this artificial world you are so real.

Don't hide your emotional existence.

In the entire universe the real you have a unique emotional essence.

Embracing your emotions just be who you are.

It's a blessing to be simple and sensitive by nature.

The world is unkind place.

No matter how much good you are, you can be always replaced.

Beware of fake people.

Try to keep yourself in a small yet trustworthy circle.

The older you get the fewer friends you can keep.

Let the real ones only stay with you being empathetic enough with your joy and grief.

My friend, you are a girl with a golden heart.

Also be your own safeguard.

Follow your intuitive rule.

Don't be an emotional fool.

Make sure, your emotions are not getting misused by the deceptive people anyway.

Don't allow anyone to color your emotional sky gray.

Your emotion has the natural beauty like the white lily in the green grass.

Your emotion makes your soul luminous.

Your emotion is scientifically true.

Your emotion has a great humane value.

Your emotion seems as pure as dawn's dew.

This world really needs the emotionally beautiful people like you.

Calmness

Amidst the chaos learn to stay calm and quiet.

Calmness always increases the probability to be right.

Being calm, you can listen to your heartfelt song.

Let your calmness make you strong.

Practice emotional independence.

Believe in the royal beauty of calmness.

No more loud words.

Let calmness be on your entire existential card.

We all are the universal dealers of both good and bad energy.

Don't let your mind get noisy.

Inhale the positive energy.

Exhale the negative energy.

Let the calmness of your mind make your inner space bright and breezy.

Let the calmness of your mind make your soul as tiny as a daisy.

Deal all in whisper.

Calmness is the basic source of mental power.

Staying calm is the highest level of self achievement
always and forever.

Let your inner sky be clear.

Let your inner weather be calm.

Don't let anyone pull you into their negativity's storm.

Let the calmness of your mind make your inner world
as beautiful as a flower farm.

Let the calmness of your mind be your ultimate charm.

Only You

Everything begins with you.

Everything ends with you and only you.

Who am I without you?

Even though you may be miles away but I only think
about you.

The oldest memory with you even seems to me so
warm and new.

Seeing the moon every night, it seems I see you.

Without you I am all alone in the worldly crew.

For the first time in my life I saw you in the
eye-kissing twilight.

It was love at first sight.

We went on a romantic date.

You seemed my inner mate.

You proposed to me on your knees.

You touched my heart just like the ocean breeze.

Your voice was like the subtle sound of the overlapping
waves.

Our love story was engrossed by destiny on the walls of a mysterious cave.

Moonlight still reminds me of your serene presence.

I love you with every living bit of my existential sense.

The smile of the moon is the echo of your laughter.

You are so near to me even being so far.

Your love is the remedy of my deepest scar.

You are my brightest human star.

Your heart is so genuine.

The sparkle of your eyes is my eternal sunshine.

It can't ever be measured how much I love you, my forever Valentine.

I read your mind just like a poet.

Thinking of you I've written so many romantic sonnets.

Your heart is inseparable from me till eternity.

Your soul is my ultimate destiny.

Your love joins my mind and body in a divine symphony.

Everything begins with you.

Everything ends with you.

My life is meaningless without you.

My love for you is like all the oceans of the multiverse
on a droplet of dew.

I just want to say you,

I love you

and only you.

The Musical Divinity

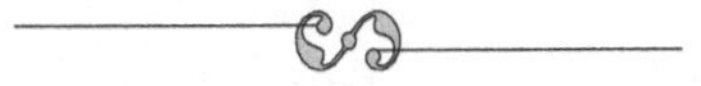

I live in the musical universe.

Deep down in my heart, the waves of a river sing a chorus.

I'm just mad over music.

Musical appeal is cosmic.

What's life without music?

Peace lies in the musical smile.

Music gradually makes the pain forgettable and fragile.

Musical fusion wipes my tears away.

A beautiful song just makes my day.

Where there is music there is absence of fear.

Let me breathe musical air.

Music is one of the deepest spiritual connections.

Let the music play on.

Musical moments are so soothing that I just stop worrying.

My veins have a forever musical fascination.

I rediscover myself through musical illumination.

Let my mind stay musically young.

Let my heart be musical in the murmuring of my
favorite songs.

Let my mood have musical relaxation.

Let my scream have musical consolation.

Music is the blessing to embrace the universal peace &
unity.

Let my soul get uplifted with the musical divinity.

Daddy-Daughter Bond

Daddy, listening to my tiny heart,

you sincerely taught me to listen to myself.

Your love dearly taught me to love my true self.

Giving enormous value to me,

you silently taught me to value my authentic self.

Being extremely kind and considerate to me,

you genuinely taught me to be kind to all.

Having immense faith on me,

you make me confident and free just like a liberated
waterfall.

There is no light without shadows.

You made me believe, even in my broken heart my
inner universe glows.

You gave the supreme importance to my wings of will
inspiring me to be self-driven.

I feel your immortal presence with the eternal sensation
of every season.

To resonate with your heartbeats, I don't need any melodious reason.

You are the single white rose in my mind's garden.

What a rosy daddy-daughter bond!

Love you for infinity and beyond.

I feel blessed with your perpetual presence.

Who am I but my father's fragrance?

The Garden of Heaven

It didn't rain for a moment in the hot summer.

Drought taught you the value of a single drop of water.

In your garden so many buds couldn't grow into flowers.

Bit by bit blooming dreams faded away,

there was almost no hope, no way.

Finally all the buds got dried and dead.

Thirsty birds forgot to sing and whistle.

Dehydrated leaves were dry and pale.

They kept falling off on the ground of an almost
lifeless garden.

You were absolutely heartbroken

and started to cry in pain.

You were bound in the disappointing chain.

The wheel of your fate was still in spin.

The garden was pale but the seed of possibility was still
a bit green.

And you started to consider everything from the
eternal perspective.

That helped you to deal with your grief.

Things also changed over time.

Nature wrote a new musical rhyme.

Flowers started to bloom again in your garden of
heaven.

You joyfully smelled the fresh floral fragrance.

You got a lesson not to lose your spirit no matter
whether your condition is dull or pleasant.

Every situation in life is temporary.

After heavy rain there is a hope of rainbow, my dearie.

Be optimistic ignoring any temporary loss or gain.

You must get butterfly's wings at the end of caterpillar's
struggle & pain.

Never put the rope at the neck of the hope.

Free yourself from the darkness of any prison.

Learn from a child how to be happy without any
reason.

Anyhow be the candle of the last hope

and keep lighting the lamps of love embracing your
kinder version.

The Universal Timeline

Our living heartbeats have stayed wavy since our birth.

Now we all have magically met each other here on this planet earth.

What a cordially coincidental warmth!

What a cosmic chance to walk together on life's seashore!

Maybe in the very next moment our living forms can't be here anymore.

We are absolutely uncertain about the span of our earthy existence.

This life seems our present tense.

Before this life all was past tense

and after this life, all will be future tense.

It's seen under eternity's lens.

In the universal timeline our entire life seems present tense.

We all are bound to earthy mortality.

But the universal timeline is for eternity.

We all are blessed with universal immortality.

Our journey is from infinity to infinity.

Beyond the limited span of the earthy breath, our time is infinite.

Realization of this cosmic truth resembles with the source of the celestial light.

Our universal journey has an eternal phase.

This life is just like a universal stoppage.

In the cosmological spectrum we are birthless and deathless

Our universal appeal is timeless.

Fool

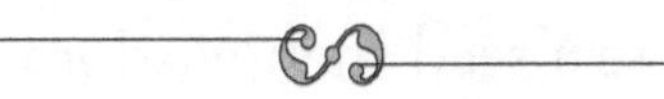

Oh, you think you can easily make others fool.

But you will eventually be trapped in your self-made ridiculous rule.

You can't make someone forever fool.

Your cunningness is surely not your intelligence.

Do you have this minimum common sense?

Your tendency to make others fool will eventually make yourself an utter stupid.

Please be shameful for your self-declared progressive speed.

Today's intelligent man is innerly molded with an old fool's clay.

Today's expert was just a novice on yesterday.

Everyone must have to be stupid at first.

It's the natural typecast.

It's easy to fool the eyes

but it's not easy to fool the heart with repeated lies.

After all we have our growing instincts.

If every fool wore a coronet then the world would be full of kings.

If foolishness were a seed then wisdom would hopefully be the tallest tree.

In the long run someone is as foolish as he wants to be.

Repeated foolishness generally comes from ignorance.

Try to vibe truth's essence.

By the way life itself makes all of us more or less fool.

To be intelligent, taking lesson from the past mistakes is obviously the most important learning tool.

As a human being you have already signed in an unseen contract paper to be occasionally fool.

So don't worry, it's cool.

If you keep asking questions, you've a very less chance to be a fool.

The real fool is generally never ever doubtful.

Anyways to be a bit more intelligent, at first you must have to be a big fool

while swimming in the universal pool.

Simplicity

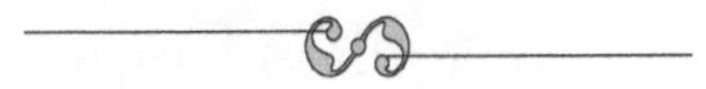

Simplicity makes our mind a starry galaxy.

Simplicity is the highest level of supremacy.

Simplicity is the heart's eternal ceremony.

Simplicity has the holiest beauty.

Amidst the negativity simple people try to live peacefully without bothering any complexity.

In the harsh reality simplicity is the rarest quality.

Simple and sensitive hearts always have to face the hardest trouble

being the easiest targets of the negative people.

With the power of simplicity they overcome all the odds just becoming more and more simple.

It's a blessing to be surrounded by simple people.

Even for the sake of your own peace, be truly simple by heart.

It's the best self-reward.

Targeting people to make them fool will never ever make anyone smart.

Any kind of true relationship is made of simplicity and trust.

Simplicity lights the million lamps in your mind.

Simplicity wisely lets you move on leaving all the baggage behind.

The more you become simple the more you become intelligent.

Simplicity keeps the things transparent.

Simplicity has an unadulterated scent.

Eventually your simplicity must help you to find your happiness quotient.

Raising My Voice against War

I am the representative of the victims in the
devastating war.

I still bear the most unfortunate people's bloody scars.

I am raising my voice against war.

War is the entire mankind's biggest enemy now, then
and forever.

War spreads the deadly poison in the air.

War is the damn spoiler of the universal peace and
tranquility.

War is the reason of terrible violence and the brutality.

War doesn't allow anyone to take a single healthy
breath in reality.

War brings the worst curse for the entire mankind.

Greed for power and money make people absolutely
blind.

The strongest man is always weaponless.

War burns the entire bridge of hope for progress.

War is the most shameful event of the human race.

Generation after generation people have to pay the cost of the sinful war.

The consequence of war is written in the ink of bloody tears.

Destroying Mother Nature's inherent bliss, war only gives us countless death and debris.

War causes infinite pain.

There is surely no gun in the earthy heaven.

War makes everyone a damn loser, sooner or later.

No one is the winner in a war.

War is the tearful story of only losers.

Let's say the biggest and the loudest 'NO' to war.

Passion

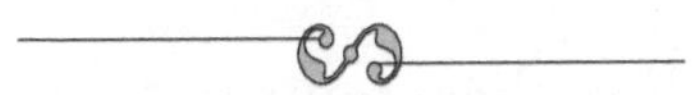

Consider the entire universal connections.

Then let your heart choose your passion.

If the passion knocks the door, bit by bit talent must be born.

Your passion is the most peaceful way to sense that you are still alive.

Life is a blissful chance to have a passionate drive.

Your passion doesn't let your tears make your inner vision blurry.

Pain is mandatory.

Your passion helps you to get rid of sufferings sooner than ever before.

Your passion lets your spirit soar.

Your passion is the source of your mental power.

Your passion eventually makes you a living wonder.

Passion is doing what you love.

Passion makes your each breath more meaningful no matter whether the phase of life is smooth or rough.

Don't let anyone steal your passion.

Your passion is your soulful recreation.

Just chase your passion.

Unapologetically live with your passion.

Your passion is your divine connection.

Your passion is the reason of your inside-out beauty.

Purity of passion must save you even from the ugliest reality.

Your passion is your soul's luminosity.

Your passion brings the fire that lights your path.

Your passion is your creative rebirth.

Your passion is the booster of your self-confidence.

Let your passion be the reason of your compassionate existence.

Your passion is the catalyst of your success.

Be intensely passionate to be boundless.

Your passion always makes you feel better.

Remember, your mental health really matters.

When it rains from your teary eyes, let your passion be your rainbow.

Just like a scintillating fountain, let you passion be your soul's inherent flow.

The War-Free World

Let the people live peacefully spreading the aroma of the universal love in the sacred air.

Let the wings of butterflies color the universe being the most natural painters.

Let the birds sing the song of harmony being the most optimistic singers.

Let the buds of peace bloom into the most fragrant flowers.

Let the leaves dance embracing love from the earthy water absorbed by root hair.

Let's light the candle of hope to remove all the nightmare of war.

Let's laugh, giggle and smile with every child deserved to have the war-free world.

For each and every child, let peace be our eternal gift of garland.

Manifest peace at core.

No more conspiracy of war behind the closed door.

Only peace can perpetually save the world not to get catastrophically pale.

Let the hope of pearly peace prevail.

58

O My Divine Lover

O my divine lover,

I meet you where the heaven meets the earth.

Love gives both of us a rebirth.

You are the smile of my gentle heart's all blooming flowers.

You truly try to make me happy in all possible ways.

Your loving presence brings serene smile even in my dull face.

Also you have the ultimate compassion for the entire human race.

You are capable to light the divine candle even in the devil's darkness.

Your inner beauty makes the universe a better place.

You make me feel endless.

You love me embracing my deepest scar.

The resonance of your love is the answer of my prayer.

The purity of your love ignites the fire of my spirit.

Cosmically you are my most precious gift

and a significant reason of my soul's spiritual uplift.

You make me feel special.

I only want to be your girl.

You weave a chain of pearls,

just for me.

Love you with all my heart, my forever dearie.

You even resonate with my unsaid wish.

You are such a celestial bliss!

My soul needs your infinite kiss.

Your love is the torchbearer to find my inner peace.

If love is real,

it makes the lovers spiritual.

True love is always divine and difficult for all of us.

O my beloved, be my most dependable shelter in the
entire universe.

Your love gives me power to break the hardest fence.

You are my lord of all heavens.

Let me convey my infinite gratitude to your purest soul.

Let's breathe and spread divine love setting it our
spiritual goal.

Reincarnation

My best friend, you were suffering from an incurable disease.

I helplessly heard your cry in the melancholic breeze.

Your fight has finally come to an end today.

The whole world looks painfully gray.

Death is so inevitable yet so unacceptable.

Hate for deadly separation is quite reasonable.

Our eternal bond of friendship is our most precious wealth.

Somehow I have to accept that you have taken your last breath.

I knew how much pain you had to bear.

Those memories were written in my broken heart with the flowing ink of tears.

Was saving your life at all possible?

Doctors said that your disease was incurable.

So I don't have any other clue; now I am all alone and blue.

But after a long time, you are sleeping peacefully.

Your face is looking so calm and flowerly.

You seem to me a floating star, so close yet so far.

Though you temporarily go away but permanently you
will never go.

Our friendship eternally grow and glow.

Universally we forever remain connected.

My colorless love for you has no chance to be faded.

Friendship is a divine connection.

There is no question of permanent separation.

We would scientifically meet via a reincarnation.

We overcome the limitations of death through this
realistic reincarnation.

Hell and heaven don't play any role as such in our
eternal participations.

My friend, eventually part of your body would
decompose in the soil.

But our togetherness wouldn't get spoiled.

One day the root of a thirsty tree would absorb the
water from that wet soil.

Then a new bud would joyfully bloom

letting me forget about losing you in the deadly gloom.

That blooming flower would surely remind me of your
smiley presence

and our friendship's divine fragrance.

We would remain the perpetual friends in the universal
fables.

To overcome the lethal trouble, power of love and
friendship makes us the undefeated rebels.

Reincarnation is the final smile over all the deadly cries.

Reincarnation is seeing the universe through the
optimistic eyes.

Reincarnation is the perpetual winner over the earthy
death.

The song of rebirth resonates with the eternal wish of
soulful depth.

Reincarnation has the enormous possibility & the
cosmic scope.

Reincarnation is the immortal story of infinite love &
hope.

Break-up

'And they lived happily ever after',

That's not the end of every romantic tale.

In the same way our break-up was inevitable.

The ship of our romantic dreams sank to the bottom of
the bay.

After break-up, gradually we could rediscover ourselves
in our separate ways.

Our broken hearts started to see the life from different
perspectives.

With the passage of time, our minds accepted our
break-up as an unavoidable grief.

The next phase was totally unknown

but we could look beyond the horizon.

Life called us separately in whisper.

Even in the gutter we could look at the stars.

Life was really kind enough to give us another chance
to be the vivid explorers.

Anyways our romance was gone with the wind
forever.

There was a severe trouble in our paradise.

Most importantly any of us was not interested to break
the ice.

Though there was a silent cry

yet as a lover, finally I had to say you an inevitable
goodbye.

When we give away love, we are the forever keepers.

Though our dreams have changed yet we still remain
the dreamers.

My dear, I was your well-wisher.

I am still your well-wisher

and will always remain your well-wisher.

Once upon a time I loved you without a doubt.

You were the treasure what my heart sought.

You were my all in all.

But our love story was ended with a teary skyfall.

After break-up it seemed, I had lost myself in the dark
forest grove.

In the wind of change, again I am able to light my
candle of hope.

Last but not least, my friend, I always wish you all the
happiness on the visit of the glorious globe.

Fragrance of Truth

Truth always has the highest priority.

Truth removes the veil from opacity.

Truth has the eternal glory.

Lack of clarity in thoughts will never let you live peacefully.

Truth is the ultimate encourager.

Truth has the supreme power.

Truth speakers always have the maximum haters.

But does it really matter to them?

Anything is prominent in truth's frame.

Always stay hungry for truthful realization of any matter.

Truth is the eye-opener.

Sometimes naked truth makes you upset.

The sun also has to face the sunset.

But a new dawn will surely smile even after the moonless night.

Truth is the most reliable friend, philosopher and guide.

Truth is the ultimate peace-maker.

We need to know the truth to be the justified thinker.

Truth teaches us the most important lesson.

Truth perpetually helps us to forget our pain.

Whenever you need to speak the truth, just don't remain silent.

Voice of truth significantly matters.

Truth is the showstopper.

Truth is the game changer.

Be honest enough to keep the clarity in your communication.

Chance of misunderstanding reduces with truthful comprehension.

Truth is the mirror in the hand of Mother Universe.

Always verify truth's signature.

Be ready to embrace any truth with your flexible nature.

Know the truth.

Grasp the truth.

Look forward with hope from the realization of truth.

Truth never limits your growth.

Truth is universally adorable.

Fragrance of truth keeps the life flowerly simple.

You Matter

Unfavorable circumstances change your outer world.

But keep your serene mind dew-pearled.

Just choose to be an authentic person in your conscientious world.

Stay away from the negative minded people.

Be wise enough to choose your circle.

People set your arbitrary values.

Just don't be blue.

Be with the genuine ones who want to see you as the winner around the globe.

Even in the darkness, let your inner eyes see the inextinguishable candle of hope.

You need self-love & considerations.

Attentively listen to your gifted intuition.

That will always help you to come out of your illusions.

To keep your inner world peaceful, you must have to follow some emotional restrictions.

You are limited edition.

Everything doesn't deserve your attention.

Give limited access of your time and energy for any reaction.

Listen to your heartfelt song.

Then just stop worrying no matter whether you have chosen right or wrong.

Be imperial.

You are special.

You matter.

Your inner voice genuinely matters.

Be the avid listener of your inner voice.

Your peace is really priceless.

Find peace within yourself even being in the random mess.

Don't take too much stress.

Give value even to the slowest progress.

Hope always leaves its trace.

Your heart is your most adorable palace.

Embrace your universally unique grace.

You are the luminous moon in your inner universe.

Let the people feel your inner beauty from the realistic terrace.

Know about the circumstantial phenomenon.

Then stand by your rational opinion.

Keep your head high and your aim even higher.

Let your golden heart glitter.

Remember, at the end of the day you matter.

Yes, you cosmically matter.

Our Favorite Actors

We all have our favorite actors.

Children also have their favorite cartoon characters.

Their tiny world emotionally vibrates with the heartbeats of those imaginary creatures.

Your favorite actor often saves your mind from real life stress and strain.

Sometimes thinking of him you even forget your pain.

This fondness of a human heart is very old and real

no matter whether your favorite character is imaginary or reel.

You truly share an amazing connection with your favorite performer.

In your inner world he eventually becomes more than an entertainer.

He becomes your wonderful friend forever.

He breathes with you just being your living dream.

His intense performance makes you so much relatable with him.

You see him beyond the lens.

You resonate with him even beyond his performance.

What an unexplainable feeling!

You are connected with him by heartstrings.

Integrating the magic of his different shades of
roles,

you feel him as a whole.

You can connect with his expressions instantly.

You get attached with him emotionally.

You'll be happy for him, sad for him, cry with him,
smile at him.

You embrace him deeply.

You communicate with him silently.

This heartiest communication keeps going on
consciously and subconsciously.

An actor has a magnificent reachability to his fans.

As a shining star, he has a magical power to remove
their minds' tans.

An actor colors his die-hard fans' world with the most
vibrant shades.

The minds of the fans turn rosy red.

At core you can feel the presence of your favorite actor just like the boy next door.

Sometimes he becomes your fantasy also through his larger than life image.

Just thinking of him, you keep writing endless fascinating passages.

You choose him directly through your heart's natural call.

Even without knowing you personally, he can vibe your love beyond the four walls of the theatre halls.

Through an actor's evolving performance, he gradually becomes your human fragrance.

Bonding with your favorite actor is really a heartfelt synchronization.

His performance can magically make your mood on.

An actor knocks your heart's door.

He gracefully enters at your heart's core letting the rhythm of your heartbeats flourish to love him more.

Finally he lives there forever

being your beloved roommate along with your smiles & tears.

A Soulful Flight

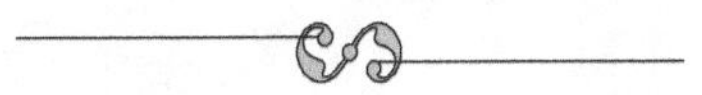

Today you strive to be a bit better human being than
what you were yesterday

just molding yourself with the past's clay.

It's not always possible to breathe the fragrant air of
flowerly spring

yet any kind of uncertainty can't stop you to fly with
your dreamy wings.

Naturally choose to be happy without any significant
rhyme or reason.

Walk with the broken.

You must blossom fully in every season.

You'll be often invited in the trap of the unnecessary
arguments.

Ignore that being calm, kind and intelligent.

Just make sure that being silent you never give your
consent to injustice.

See the thing as it is without any prejudice.

Choose to speak when your words are justified,
compassionate and truthful.

Choose to be logical, straightforward and cool.

Your heart dearly needs your hug and kiss.

Choosing peace over anything is the most healthy
lifestyle practice.

Be forgiving and simple.

You are the pebble in the pond that helps to create
hope's ripples.

Be a soulful performer in the universal stage.

Learning has no age.

Feed your mind with knowledge, not garbage.

Then keep increasing the level of your knowledge.

Turn your depth of knowledge into wisdom.

You must blossom.

As a blooming flower,

you keep spreading natural fragrance without hiding
your true color.

Don't participate in any worthless fight.

Let self empowering wisdom be your divine guide.

Embrace your inner moonlight.
You were born to choose a soulful flight.

The Musical Dance

My darling, our souls meet in a musical moment.

The dance of our heartbeats spreads the celestial scent.

Now my eyes don't want to lose you even for a single glance.

We dream together to make our romantic journey as beautiful as a musical dance.

We celebrate the aroma of creative resonance.

Musical dance spreads the mind-blowing fragrance.

Let the melodious music play.

Let our auspicious souls sway.

Let the warmth of the musical dance melt our hearts.

Music is such a divine art.

Music is our minds' magnet.

Musical dance makes us believe, there is no lock, no bolt and even no gate.

Love is the holiest connection.

Let's write our love story in musical notation.

Music and dance together make the magical fusion.

Musical dance is the eternal devotion.

Music resonates with the true spirit of Mother Nature.

Oh darling, you dance like a wavy river.

You dance like an earthy angel.

Musical dance can make a packed heaven and an empty hell.

Musical dance gives us the spiritual uplift in the midst of the chaotic crowd.

My sweetheart, you dance like a peacock in love witnessing the rainy cloud.

Your dance is as spontaneous as a flawless fountain.

Let the music clear our minds' all the stains.

Let the music mingle with dance to Mother Nature's core.

Let's start our musical dance to live once more.

Emotional Control

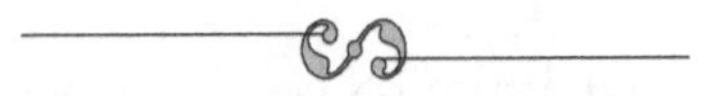

Never give the power to anyone to be your emotional controller.

Your emotional controller will be eventually your abuser

and your energy sucker.

If you cross the danger line,

you may have to lose your sunshine.

Don't trust anyone blindly.

Don't be so silly.

Set a healthy boundary.

If you don't want to get lost,

Just don't get absolutely attached with anyone at any cost.

Don't let anyone take any undue advantage.

Be a cautious performer at the real life stage.

A repeated mistake is nothing but a choice.

Don't lament for your past relationship.

You were surely in the wrong trip.

Don't be a blind lover anymore.

Blind love eventually hurts to the core.

A crazy lover must have to be disappointed someday.

Don't let the absolute dependence be the emotional
food of your tray.

If the water of love becomes too much salty,

Even being thirsty, just stop drinking it not to give any
serious penalty.

Emotional control is vital.

It's a safe mode of survival.

You are only responsible to keep your sensitive heart
safe.

You have to face the up and down movements of so
many emotional waves.

A rough sea always made an expert sailor.

Be your own emotional controller.

You can't control the outside matters.

Limit your reactions for other's behavior.

Emotionally protect yourself.

Let your brain instruct your heart to defend yourself.

Don't let anyone make your inner world pale.

Under any circumstances, don't ever let anyone make your life hell.

Believe in the evergreen story of fairy tale.

But never get lost in the midst of the vampires & the evil crew.

Never allow anyone to take your magic stick away from you.

My Dear Friend

We were two flowers in the same petiole, my dear.

We breathed the same air.

We shared our every bit of smile and tears.

We wandered in our very own mysterious world.

Sometimes we got into brawl.

But often we were flooded in amicable joy.

Anyways we all would ultimately have to be the destiny's toy.

I used to talk to you with all my heart.

I listened to you with all my soul.

I could even read your silence.

I could fondly find myself in your very dear existence.

But just like beautiful flowers get dried, beautiful days are also gone too soon.

Even being far from full, true friendship is always the same moon.

In the inevitable darkness of life, we parted ways suddenly.

Thinking of you, ceaseless tears still make my vision all blurry.

Is it ever possible to get buried the evocative memory of such a loving friendship?

Where is the end of this enormous grief?

Oh my dear friend, I miss you, I miss you, I miss you very badly.

My earthy eyes find you daily.

Tears roll down my eyes every now and then.

My friend, do you also feel the same pain?

When can I hear your sweet voice again?

It was the most pleasing audible sense in my brain.

When can I see your unforgettable face again?

While playing barefoot on the ground we were as happy as the green grass.

You were my best friend in the universal class.

You were always right beside me to protest against anyone's tease.

We woke up listening to the song of the morning breeze.

Our friendship has the open sky full of stars.

But happiness doesn't last forever.

One stormy night we came to a teary split-up in the jaw of the deadly war.

Years gone still I have been finding you madly here and there.

Even being separated from you, my soul still bears an enormous pain.

I can still feel your unconditional love in my veins.

Our friendly hearts together wished to have a lifetime trip.

We are still connected with each other by the invisible thread of love & friendship.

Our bond is the eternal sunshine, a friendship as green as a pine.

A true friend like you is rarest of rare.

We were born to be destined together.

Our wait will soon be over

and we will surely meet again, my dear.

The Universal Science Gallery

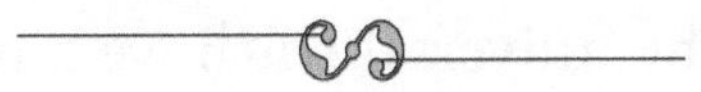

The root of every truth must have a scientific smell.

Scientific truth is hidden in each and every biological cell.

The smallest particle of an element is called an atom.

An average human cell typically has hundred trillion atoms.

We live in the universe of atoms.

We all are the children of cosmos.

Our universal journey is really incredible.

Atoms are chemically indestructible.

Atoms are made of protons, neutrons and electrons

those can be simply rearranged but can't be destroyed by a chemical reaction.

But atoms are destructible through nuclear reactions.

Let our scientific minds get flourished.

The stunning universe includes the land, air, water, earth, sun, moon, stars and the galaxies.

Let's be the witness of the cosmic truth from the universal science gallery.

To know the universal truth we have to think scientifically and rationally.

We all are the nature's wonderful creatures.

We are biologically blessed with unique features.

Science is our past, present and the future.

Everything can be explained by the law of nature.

How interestingly the Big Bang theory describes the origin of universal rapture!

The universe massively expanded from an initial state of high density and temperature.

Various cosmological models of Big Bang explain the evolution of the universe.

Many more cosmic truth is yet to be revealed to us.

Million years ago,

our oldest ancestor, the single-celled organism, was born on this planet earth.

Thereafter evolution has crossed a long path.

Over time, evolution brings the changes in the genetic diversity of population.

We all are the result of million years of evolution.

A must read theory, Charles Darwin's theory of
evolution by natural selection.

We all have atomic structure.

We all are blessed with cosmic power.

We are made of star stuff.

The journey of life can be wonderfully expressed
through an evolutionary graph.

Calcium in our bones, nitrogen in our DNA, iron in
our blood all are contributed by star stuff.

We may have our deep scars

but cosmologically we all are the born stars.

Tea Break

Every morning life gives us a new chance to start a fresh day with a cup of tea.

A cup of hot tea is the ticket from the drowsiness to the normality.

A cup of tea is my happiness key.

Friends, next time, don't forget to invite me in your tea party.

Whenever it comes to tea, I'm its true devotee.

What's a life without a cup of tea?

If there is a cup of tea, there is a ray of hope.

My soul belongs to tea no matter whether my body is in Asia or Europe.

I laugh at my broken heart sipping a cup of hot tea.

A cup of tea just makes my inner spirit free.

Aura of me-time is incomplete without the crispy snacks & a cup of hot tea.

A cup of tea makes me feel the queen in my inner kingdom.

A cup of tea is my liquid wisdom.

Whenever you ask me to have tea, my answer is always,
'Yes'.

A cup of tea keeps my mind, mood and body fresh.

A cup of tea relieves my pain.

A cup of tea is my oxygen.

Without tea I just can't survive.

Tea makes me feel so much alive.

No one feels alone with a cup of tea surely.

Even when I was a little kid I demanded to have tea
regularly.

At first my parents tactfully gifted me a small cup to
limit my tea intake.

Without tea, life would be a mistake.

Sometimes I get wonder,

is my blood made of tea, dear?

Hello, I'm seriously asking you so, it's not my funny
bone's humor.

Take your time to think deeper

and reply me later.

Now let me have a tea break.

Let me sip my tea with rich butter cake.

Let me feel the organic essence of the tea leaf.

A cup of tea is my inseparable partner in both joy and grief.

Tea definitely helps me to stay positive.

So I'm quite responsive

that my blood group is tea positive.

The Joker

With each passing day, we are losing more natural beauty.

What a pathetic reality!

Our greed is really ugly.

We've been coloring the world artificially.

Now the world becomes a biased place.

Money and power are all what people chase.

Biasness makes the life a big joke.

Now what can be the masterstroke?

To keep smiling in this biased reality, you have to be nothing but a joker.

Otherwise people's sufferings hopelessly make you a sad soul forever.

Being optimistic, you choose to bring smile in people's faces with empathy and humor.

To make others smiley, you have to learn to smile at first, my dear.

Now blowing in the wind I also become a joker

and promise to make you feel smiley forever.

Sooner or later, no one can stop life to be a real mess.

My heart was also broken into hundreds of pieces.

Anyways I gathered my bleeding heart's all the broken
pieces.

Bit by bit I sticked them back together.

Even now you can see all the scars.

But very wonderfully my wounded heart is still reliable.

Empathy is still alive in my heart's kernel.

And forever it will be there, my darling.

I am a joker but I will never joke on people's feelings.

I always choose to find silver lining.

I have a cool mind-set, dear.

I always remember that I'm a joker.

Yes, I am nothing but a joker.

My tears even try to keep you smiley forever.

My mind is a green nursery.

Reality tries to make me believe, life is full of misery.

But laughing at reality, I myself believe, life is not a
tragedy.

If you want to dance in rain, just don't be afraid of getting muddy.

The entire universe is your buddy.

Life is nothing but a comedy.

So what it's a tragic comedy?

Sleep Therapy

Sleep therapy is the best ever therapy.

A sound sleep is a lifestyle wellness trophy.

Sleeping is the most soothing meditation.

Bed is the most wanted place for relaxation.

If we are too much tired, sound sleep is the ultimate solution.

In our adulthood nap seems a vacation.

whereas in our childhood nap was a punishment.

A sound sleep at night makes our morning melody more pleasant.

Bed is our most cozy shelter.

Bed is a friend forever

and also the witness of our every dream.

Our bond with the blankets is passionately warm.

Let me sleep on the lap of the bed ignoring life's all the storms.

In the garden of the sky, flowerly stars are dreamily twinkling.

Beauty of the blooming moon is just breathtaking.

My consciousness wants to drown in the sleeping sea.

Mother Universe is lullabying me.

Starry dreams are closing my sleepy eyes.

Good night, guys.

Deep Understanding

There is something beyond pass and fail.

Deep understanding increases that acceptance level.

Deep understanding comes with flexible attitude.

In the midst of all the chaos, deep understanding lets you find your own solitude

that eventually gives you all the answers.

Why, what, who, how, when, where, all become gradually clear.

Deep understanding often makes you a forgiver.

Deep understanding makes you a constant learner.

Deep understanding helps you to find your best friend just looking at the mirror.

Don't ever ask yourself, 'How can someone be so fake?'

It's just your primary responsibility not to trust a snake.

Expectations from the people must be lower than the lowest.

Just get up, dress up and learn to celebrate your messy life like a fest.

Deep understanding never lets you beg for anyone's attention repeatedly.

Deep understanding brings the clarity that helps you to realize the truth naturally.

Deep understanding considers both side of the story.

Deep understanding is your brain's most adorable glory.

All is ok as long as you don't have to deal with extreme pain.

Deep understanding never ever lets you fight for the small gain.

Deep understanding only allows the peaceful indulgence of your brain.

Deep understanding is a regular practice.

The path of deep understanding leads you to equitable justice.

To understand anything deeper than ever before,

you have to listen to your heartfelt brain's core.

Stay Tuned

Let's breathe love in the musical air.

Let's dance together now and forever.

Let the musical dance make us believe that any pain
finally doesn't matter.

Let's dance forgetting everything.

Let's be rhythmic with the anklets' tuning.

Let's dance with the stormy wind.

Let the innocence of our childhood rewind.

Let's feel the melodious lyrics.

Dance is the visual music.

Let's dance to embrace Mother Universe.

Let's dance with the breath of music having the artistic
joy of Venus.

Let's dance on the pearly moon.

It's time to stay tuned.

Let's dance with all our souls.

Let's live without making any intentional foul.

Dancers and singers have invisible wings to fly.

Let's dance on the sacred soil sensing the touch of the starry sky.

Let's forget, one day all of us will die.

Music and dance are the most lively expressions of truth.

Let's make the unfair reality musically peaceful and smooth.

Mood Swings

Learn to handle your mood swings

no matter whether your mind is caught in a winter blizzard or enjoying colorful spring.

You can control your mood swings without telling yourself any lies.

Settlement with the naked truth is the ultimate peacemaker in your mind's paradise.

You've to handle your mood swings being practical.

Follow the raw truth's unbiased signal.

Get intelligently attached with the realistic string.

Being brutally honest to yourself, you've to identify the accurate reason of your mood swings.

Most of the problems are not hard enough to make you mentally lame.

After analyzing all, find the root cause of the problem.

If possible, try to bring the change

otherwise channelize your acceptance range.

Think about the alternative options.

Under any circumstances you have to choose an optimal solution.

The chance of mood swings is directly proportionate with expectation.

So just no more expectation,

grasp this truthful realization.

You've to handle your own mood off.

Priority for self love must be on the top.

Remember, no one is responsible to keep your mood on.

Be your own heart's most wanted and coolest companion.

Be positive, stay active.

Have a sound sleep.

Don't live in the past's grief.

Nature has so much to say.

Listen to nature at least once in a day.

Your heart is eternally worthy.

Your food plate must be healthy.

Sometimes treat yourself with your favorite food.

You must feel good.

Take the help of your hobbies to boost your mood.

It's quite expected that the voice of reality would be often rude.

Just never ever be rude to yourself.

Take utmost care of your inner self.

Too much mood swings are the threats.

It's an enemy at the gate.

You may lose the balance to deal with your daily life's commitments.

In extreme case you must have to consult a psychiatrist.

Medical science surely helps you to get rid of your mind's mist.

Normal mood swings are part and parcel of everyday life.

A bit emotional up-down is not needed to be cut by any metaphorical knife.

Be highly responsible to keep your mood good to have an emotionally peaceful drive.

Valentine's Day

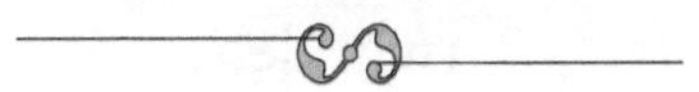

Today is Valentine's Day.

That makes lovers' hearts sway.

One of the most famous restaurants in a small town is full of couples.

What a romantically delicious smell!

Here a beautiful lady comes alone.

In her personal life she has recently faced a cyclone.

She orders her favorite food.

Her dopamine and serotonin hormones make her feel good.

The lady is enjoying her own solitude.

This Valentine's Day is very special for her.

She has been free from all the emotional baggage of relationship so far.

It's really soothing; it seems to her the most sizzling spring.

Raw flavor of singlehood is really awesome.

She can feel her own heart's warm.

What an addictive charm!

Her face is no longer pale; her big black eyes
twinkle.

Her heart is no longer anyone's toy.

She is not looking for any instant joy,

she just wants to stay indifferent from any kind of
pain.

Right now romantically she is not thinking to mingle
with someone again.

She wants to enjoy her much-awaited singlehood.

She is in a very relaxed mood.

She finds the way to her inner paradise.

She learns to value anything that sustains her peace.

From the very beginning she was honest enough in the
relationship.

But the wound was getting more and more deep.

Finally lack of trust couldn't save that relationship
anyway.

It's time to mould her heart with new hope's clay.

It's time to start her post-breakup solo trip.

Her partner was quite abusive.

Moreover lack of transparency made the relationship toxic.

Right now she is missing no one.

Her sky is clear enough to smile again with the sun.

No more argument, no more quarreling.

Today she is truly her own darling.

Sometimes no feeling for someone is the best feeling.

For a broken heart, it's mentally healthy.

The lady believes, no matter what happens in life, each breath is worthy.

May the life of that optimistic lady be more meaningful.

She was not born to live with any unjust rule.

She deserves peace and happiness.

Wish her a wider smile with a scintillating grace.

No more toxicity, it's time to celebrate her inner serenity.

Now she is blessed with an emotionally independent shine.

Today she is her very own Valentine.

The Learning Sky

Life goes on just changing the themes.

You've to live and die many times in a single lifetime.

When you are reborn, you try to learn not to be
squeezed again like a lime.

You are in a recursive learning process.

Can you feel that eternal grace?

You were born, you died.

You were reborn and flied.

But again you died.

Nothing to mourn,

again you were born.

Now you keep flying in the learning sky.

In each rebirth, your newborn heart hopefully
whispers, 'Baby, you can do all, just one more try'.

Then even being broken, you choose not to cry.

Your wings also become a bit more powerful to fly.

Death opens the gate of a new life to dream high and
fly beyond the sky.

A single life evolves with countless rebirths before
saying the final goodbye.

Life is a one-time gift.

The process of learning and unlearning uplifts you bit
by bit.

Listen to your heartbeats from eternity's core.

Feel, the entire universe wants to let your spirit soar.

In each rebirth, you fly more high in the learning sky
than ever before.

Beware of a Liar

Beware of a liar.

A liar is the spoiler of spoilers.

Lie is the nightmare.

Let your brain be the truth-seeker

no matter whether the truth is simply sweet or unapologetically bitter.

Once a liar always a liar.

If someone is caught red-handed for lying,

just don't trust him anymore

and seal your door.

Sooner or later, truth is all what you must have to be ready to accept.

Truthful knowledge is the most powerful asset.

Being practical check all the facts.

Without knowing the actual truth, don't just assumedly react.

Truth is colorlessly colorful.

Nothing is more beautiful than being truthful.

Let your heart be the plain land of truth no matter whether the path of reality is rough or smooth.

Half-truth is the most dangerous lie.

A liar wrongly paints your dreamy sky.

It's hard to digest the nasty lie.

To know the truth, you must have to be a realistic thinker.

Beware of a liar.

A liar can put you anywhere.

Run away from a liar, the sooner the better.

Lie has no future.

Only truth can hopefully reach the final destination.

Peace comes with a truthful clarification.

A liar's paradise is made of glass.

The entry point of the ultimate peace needs truth's gate-pass.

Music Therapy

Stay blessed with music therapy.

Let your stormy mind be musically peaceful and happy.

Let the ocean in your heart be beautified by the musical pearls.

Let the music therapy make your inner garden melodically floral.

Every time you listen a beautiful song, you are reborn with a new musical mould.

Let all the musical petals of your soul and mind unfold.

Let the lyrical thoughts make you beautiful and bold.

Let the blood in your veins be blessed to have a musical flow.

Let your inner eyes grasp the colors of the musical rainbow.

Let the music therapy help you to take a deep musical breath.

Let the music therapy save you from the gradual deterioration of mental health.

Music is the most deeply felt magic.

Music therapy gives you a lifetime support for not being mentally sick.

Music is the higher revelation than any philosophy.

To stay tuned with cosmic energy, embrace music therapy.

Blood Donation

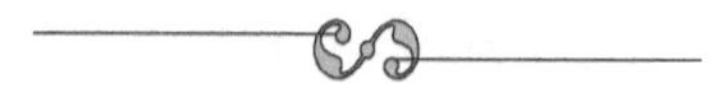

The curse of racism makes us blind.

Caste based discrimination is the most shameful issue for the entire mankind.

What's the caste, creed, race or religion of blood?

Blood is too pure to have a caste or religion.

Our skin, flesh and bones are also too natural to have any kind of man-made division.

We have the same blood in our veins.

The evil men try to break the bond of humanity every now and then.

They try to build the walls of racism spreading hatred and detestation.

Let's feel everything just being human no matter what's our caste, creed, race or religion.

Somewhere someone is crying in the sickbed.

Bit by bit his hope for staying alive is just getting faded.

Death is almost on his destiny's card.

He is struggling to take his each breath for the most urgent need of blood.

All other efforts to save him have already failed.

Amidst the terrible darkness you can be the light of a miracle.

Your donated blood can save his life.

Donating blood is having a spiritual drive.

Do the racists only ask for the blood of their own religion at blood bank to save their loved one's life?

Scientifically, there are so many health benefits for regular blood donation.

To avoid the future medical complicacy for the next generation,

a few blood tests must be mandatory before initiating any matrimonial relationship.

Today's alertness can prevent tomorrow's grief.

Beware of blood-borne diseases like Hepatitis B, HIV/ AIDS.

More programs are needed to be arranged on health awareness.

A single drop of blood has enormous possibility to create an ocean of happiness.

Blood donation is one of the holiest contributions.

Blood donation deserves universal admiration.

Blood donation is a social responsibility.

Blood donation is a moral duty.

A single drop of blood brings million hopes and living aspirations.

A blood donor gets uplifted to a soulful illumination.

A blood donor is a cosmic healer.

A blood donor is a divine helper.

A blood donor and a blood infuser are blessed to be each other's friends from vein to vein.

A blood donation camp is a holy initiative in the earthy heaven.

A donor can also donate blood visiting blood bank.

A blood donor shines in the top humane rank.

Blood donation makes a donor's blood divine.

A blood donor is the human sunshine.

Every time you donate blood, you are someone's lifesaver.

Every time you donate blood, you are in someone's prayer.

The Bed

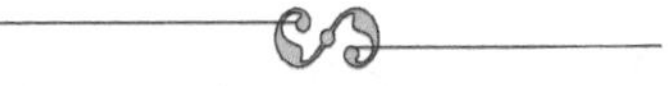

It's time to go to bed.

Everything will be silent soon in our heads.

One of the most attractive objects in a room is nothing but the cozy bed.

If the bed is wrapped in a decorative bedcover,

it becomes the entire room's beauty enhancer.

Beauty of the room is also our mood-booster.

Soft pillow is one of the most innocent non-living creatures.

We want to sink into the pillows.

Beauty sleep is the secret of our glow.

Being nonjudgmental, wet pillows know all the untold stories of our broken hearts.

We can tell them our top secrets without any need of staying alert.

If we sleep eight hours daily,

We spend one third of our life in a peaceful sleeping valley.

Oh, what a blessing!

Sleeping has the magical power of healing.

Nap is the happy hour.

Sleeping is a lifesaving drug always and forever

and bed is without doubt the most wanted dealer.

Eye Donation

Keep your eyes wide to enjoy the most delightful sense of sight.

Eyes make you feel the difference between darkness & light.

Eyes are the windows of the colorful universe.

Blindness is the most terrible curse.

Your sense of sight is no doubt the cosmic rapture.

Eyes make you mesmerized showing the beauty of Mother Nature.

Your sense of sight makes you the hopeful witness of every sunrise.

Is there anything more precious than eyes?

Think about the people who can't see anything.

Then just closing your eyes, try to do something,

You can vibe the enormous hardships & pain of those blind people.

You can feel their endless struggle.

Those unfortunates are punished without any wickedness.

Is there any way to make them forever free from the
curse of blindness?

Is it possible to bring their sighted existence anyway on
this planet earth?

If possible, it must be a rebirth.

And yes, it's infinitely possible.

Oh my bright-eyed friends, you can be the miracles.

Steps are really simple.

Take an immensely hopeful pledge to donate your eyes
after your death.

Oh, what a humane inheritance of biological wealth!

What a divine gift!

The entire universe must be filled with hopeful light.

Someday your donated eyes would help the blind
people to have their sense of sights.

Their reborn eyes would be the witnesses of the divine
beauty of the universe.

It would be the end of a terrible curse.

Researchers also need donated eye tissues to develop
new treatment of cataracts, glaucoma and many other
conditions.

Eye donation is the most sacred donation.

Use your magical power to provide blind people's visions.

Since I took the pledge for eye donation,

smile of Mother Universe has seemed brighter than ever before.

Oh, what an eternal surprise at cosmic core!

What a scientific bliss!

My dear friends, you would have to take a prompt action just after my death to fulfill my soulful wish.

You would have to call to the nearby eye bank for the collection of my donated eyes.

I soulfully thank you all in advance, my friends.

Let's prove that the death is not the end.

Let's dream to make a world free from blindness.

Let it be the mission for vision of human race.

All what we need for eye donation is the blessing of science and the social awareness.

My dear listeners, I beg you to take the pledge to donate your earthy eyes

and stay alive even after your death to see the flowerly world twice.

Health Is Wealth

Good health makes you feel beautiful inside and out.

Good health helps you to grow to the deeper root.

Always try to follow the healthy lifestyle rules.

Ignoring health you only make yourself the real fool.

Your health is your most valuable asset.

Deteriorated health condition eventually brings all the regrets.

Any work can't be performed without your mental and physical labor.

For a standard performance, good health is the most significant contributor.

Stay healthy to respond to your life's call.

Stay healthy to focus on your goal.

Breaking the silence of the valley, breathe deep.

Good night, have a sound sleep.

After a few hours wake-up alarm rings; beep, beep.

Are you sure that you've got sufficient sleep?

If yes, just go for a morning walk.

Trust me; you rock.

Health is wealth.

Money can't buy anyone's health.

But money is mandatory for a standard living.

Good health is the greatest blessing.

Just like physical health, mental health also enormously matters.

Take care of your mind, body and soul always and forever.

Eat nutritious foods to stay healthy.

Your good health is the primary condition to make you wealthy.

No man can be happy on a hungry stomach.

Health depends on your genetics, lifestyle and luck.

Sickness teaches you the real worth of your health.

Nothing is more precious than your healthy breath.

Your brain is fertile soil; your dream is the rain.

Your body is your garden.

You are the gardener.

Your wishes are the fruits and the flowers.

Your soul is the delicate scent of jasmine.

Your mindful thoughts are evergreen.

Let every hopeful dawn welcome the new sunshine

whispering in your ears, 'Oh friend, stay healthy, fit
and fine'.

Accept the Truth

Truth is the cosmic light.

Truth doesn't change just because you can't stomach it.

Truth is followed by logical rules.

Sometimes silence is the best answer to the fool.

Lie's comfort is temporary.

Accept the truth even if it's scary.

Only truth can save your heart permanently.

Truth has an irreplaceable glory.

Face the truth to be a real warrior.

So what if the truth is even not in your favor?

Yet dig the truth for gaining the ultimate mental power.

The light of truth is the real torchbearer.

Sometimes the naked truth makes your wound acute

yet accept the truth existing in the deepest root.

Be ready to burn with the truth.

Then like a phoenix you spread the wings and rise from your ashes to be blessed with an emotional rebirth.

Be the human embodiment of truth to gain the power of controlling your own mind.

Just like the dust, soon all the pain will be gone with the wind.

A Prisoner in a Zoo

I'm a wild monkey.

But I am very unlucky.

I'm a prisoner in a zoo.

What's my sin? No clue.

Earlier I lived my life with natural joy.

While climbing on trees, stems were my toys.

I was absolutely free.

I used to jump from tree to tree.

Now I can't do so.

I have no freedom from my head to toe.

Oh men, your conspiracies make me a prisoner.

I haven't done any sin yet I have been punished like a
sinner.

Don't I deserve freedom other than some food for
lunch and dinner?

Can't I ever meet my friends and family members?

Can't I wander anymore?

I wish I could break the prison door.

You make me feel absolutely loner.

I am drowning in the ocean of tears.

Visitors of the zoo laugh at me making fun every now
and then.

No one can ever imagine my enormous pain.

I am an innocent animal.

I was born to grasp nature's smell.

I'm unjustly imprisoned in a jail.

It's so nasty.

Oh men, don't you feel guilty?

How can you demand yourself the most intelligent
animal on this planet?

You are just the heartless species.

Who the hell are you to make me a prisoner?

You are nothing but the brutal oppressors.

I haven't breathed well since the loss of my freedom.

Taking away my birthright, you are violating life's basic
norm.

Now I'm a bit down but I'm sure, I will get back my
form.

Then what if I make you the prisoners?

But deep down I want to abolish all the zoos forever.

Men, you misuse your power.

Just giving me some food you think, my all other
wishes are over.

You are the real sinners.

Oh, let me see the sky.

Otherwise mentally I will soon die.

Oh men, you are so cruel.

You make my life hell.

Injustice must have to end after a certain phase.

Time will take all the revenge.

Beware of the curse of Mother Nature.

On earth Newton's third law naturally vibes
everywhere.

Purity of deeds will be the ultimate winner.

I will not be helpless forever.

Because of you now I'm at my worst.

Someday I will surely blast.

Your all conspiraies will be finished on that day.

Rectify your mistake before drowning in the consequential bay.

Injustice can't have the last smile.

The nasty power of cruelty is fragile.

I will fight to be free forever.

The day of my independence is not so far.

Just keep watching me.

My willpower will make me forever free.

Mother Nature has blessed me to be the ultimate winner.

I will again live my wildlife grasping all the natural colors & flavors.

My Inner Peace

There was a time when I wanted to be the winner of
every race.

Then I realized, self accomplishment truly lies in inner
peace

and I don't always need to be in the spotlight.

Now my eyes are widely open with divine touch of
spiritual light.

My inner sight makes me believe,

peace is as promising as a bare tree's first born
leaf.

My conscience makes me clear,

my inner peace is my ultimate healer.

It seems, I'm the spiritual child of the peaceful moon
raised by the illuminated stars.

Amidst the chaos, I find peace in my heart.

I want to be the oasis in the desert.

Peace is universally the most adorable gift.

If my path gives me peace, the path is right.

A bit peace is now much more important than winning
all the fights.

Oh my Mother Universe, let me be my own light,

please uplift my spirit.

Bless me to have a perpetually peaceful mind.

I am just the dust; you are my divine wind.

What is success without inner peace?

Peace is the heavenly bliss.

Where there is justice there is peace.

Let my soul rise.

Time flies resonating with the truth, our graves will be
of the same size.

No more wish to toss the dice.

I just want to have the eternal peace.

Enough is enough.

Now my inner peace is more solicited than any success
depicted in the curve graph.

My power is all about my emotional control.

The ultimate source of my inner peace lies in the
serenity of my soul.

Be Choosy

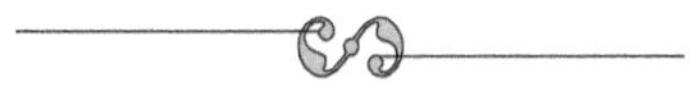

Let your heart choose to be kind and humble.

Let your mind choose to be friendly and simple.

Be choosy to get emotionally attached with people.

Keep yourself in a positive circle.

Your proper choice would only save your smiley
dimple.

Your choice would decide whether your sky would be
gray or purple.

Your right choice wouldn't let your happiness get
disappeared like a bubble.

By the way, if the wrong choice destroys your inner
peace, don't waste your time to say it goodbye.

Give yourself another chance to repaint your sky.

Like melting snow you wash yourself of yourself.

Make the most genuine friendship with your inner
self.

Then listen to your truest self.

You can't change anyone's toxic behavior.

But you can choose to get mentally detached from that abuser.

Don't ever afford apathy.

Don't choose someone who makes you feel unworthy.

No one is that important for sure.

Choose yourself to be your own cure.

You also have some limits.

If you can't change something, you've to endure it.

Choose to do something with utmost clarity.

Give your inner peace the highest priority.

When you choose the inputs and procedures, think about the probable outputs also.

Your choice decides your direction of flow.

Flowing in the right direction you can grow.

Choose peace over everything.

Without peace you can't truly achieve anything.

For your every choice, keep balance between your heart and brain.

The consequence of your choice would be loaded on your own shoulder's crane.

To know the truth, choose to be an enduring observer

and be ready to go too far.

You must have to wait to get all the answers.

Choose to accept time's inevitable limitations.

Be choosy to take all kind of life-changing decisions.

Be choosy to uplift your higher self connection.

Be choosy to explore your soulful illumination.

If you have all options, be choosy.

If you have only two options, be choosy.

Yes, always choose to be choosy.

Then, and only then, even being in the thorns of the outer world, you can make your inner world rosy.

The Dream

Believe in the beauty of your dream

that has the charm of the moonbeam.

Let your dream flow like an overwhelming stream.

The burble of the stream reminds you of the heartbeats
of your dream.

Be the sleepless dreamer.

Your dream plants the seeds of your future.

Your dream is bigger than your all fears.

Your dream has no expiry date.

Your dream is more powerful than the uncertain fate.

Your dream is more powerful than the harshest
reality.

Your dream gives you the wings to fly with enormous
possibility.

In the paradise of your mind, all the golden dreams
beautifully glitter.

Your courage to pursue your dream is the most
important factor.

No matter who says what, just chase your dream, my dear.

Your all dreams are valid.

Any heartbeat is free enough to see the dream be it of an old lady or a small kid.

Think big, dream big, believe big.

Work hard.

Let your growing wisdom be your safeguard.

Keep faith on your dreamy wings just like a bird.

Sooner or later, you must get your reward.

Your dream eventually reveals your opportunity.

Be action oriented for the accomplishment of your dream with universal hope and possibility.

Your dream is your creative version for the future.

Be an awakening dreamer.

Someday You will surely reach for the stars.

Experience

Each and every work has its unique spark.

Experience is the priceless gift for any worker.

Works seem the buds opening into the flowers

whereas experience seems the fragrance of those flowers.

Experience is the best tutor.

Experience really matters.

Experience prominently makes the difference.

Experience helps us to cross the most challenging fence.

Experience helps us to strive for excellence.

While experiencing life we have to fail again and again.

Sometimes we have to deal with the extreme pain.

But our pain is our fuel.

This fuel helps us to drive the solace of our soul.

Experience gradually makes our nerve strong.

Experience intuitively helps us to understand what's going wrong.

Experience helps us not to repeat the same mistake.

Being more experienced, we cut one more happy birthday cake.

Then thinking of our silly mistakes of the past, we just laugh.

Experience helps us to make our life a bit less tough.

Experience is a cumulative growth process.

Experience is the key of future success.

Experience leads us to the deeper sense.

Each breath gives us a cosmic opportunity to gain more experience.

It seems each drop of labor of the entire mankind makes a holy river.

Experience is the water vapor generated from that river water.

Success is the rainfall.

No work is small.

Aging of experience is phenomenal.

Even being all broken, experience doesn't let you get bent.

If work is the burning flame of an aromatic candle,
experience is its wonderful scent

that can't be seen, only felt.

We all were born to be the eternal learners.

Experience is the teacher of teachers.

You Are Undefined

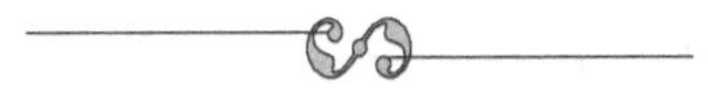

You can't be defined by your qualification, job, status or money.

You are deeper than anyone's judgmental theory.

You can't be defined by your caste, creed, religion, race, age, looks or gender.

It's not possible to define you just through some parameters.

You are undefined till eternity.

You are the integral part of infinity.

Celebrate your unique individuality.

Some people always do judgments.

Those judgmental people just deprive themselves from the cosmic merriments.

Life is too short to pay unnecessary attention to the source of negativity.

Recharge yourself with the blessings of cosmic positivity.

You are gifted with celestial opportunity.

You can't be restricted by any definer's limitations.

Your infinite mind can't possibly have any finite definition.

You are momentarily reborn with a new sensation.

Rediscover yourself with new resolutions.

You are absolutely undefined on the universal canvas.

No matter who you are, abstractly you have a heart big enough to hold the entire universe.

Love Yourself

My baby, you were born to love yourself.

Stay tuned to the melody of your true self.

Keep your heart warm and head cool.

You are the easiest target to make yourself fool.

Removing all the veils from your eyes, find your true self.

Forgetting all the man-made limitations, free yourself.

Deeply fall in love with yourself.

Be your loyal lover first and foremost.

That needs no extra cost.

Then even if you are a wanderer, you just don't get lost.

Find peaceful light within your innermost self.

Feel the entire universe within yourself.

If you can love yourself then only you can get the spirit to love others.

Love yourself like a tree loves its flowers.

Love yourself like the night sky loves the stars.

Give affection to your inner child as if you are your own mother.

Adore yourself just like a daughter adores her father.

Appreciate yourself just like a farmer appreciates the rain after the drought.

Don't leave the battlefield all of a sudden just remembering how bravely you've still fought.

Save yourself just like the roots try to save the tree till the end of the furious storm.

Listen to your heartfelt norms.

Give importance to you just like life gives importance to oxygen.

Take care of your health giving the silent thanks to the antibodies for fighting against the antigens.

My dear, while finding true love,

don't forget to see the person smiling at you in the mirror.

Your heart is your divine shelter.

Be your true love forever.

Let's take a look on the survival strategy.

Life's most important truth,

no one can ultimately save you but yourself.

Life's most valuable advice,

believe in yourself.

Last but not least, life's holiest chant,

love yourself, love yourself and love yourself.